"Money is only a tool.
It will take you wherever you wish,
but it will not replace you as the driver."

~Ayn Rand

Your Personal Money Diary
TABLE OF CONTENTS

Your Personal
MONEY DIARY
Introduction

As a Personal Money Trainer, I have seen firsthand the importance of knowing what you have, what you need and what your money goals are. When it comes to planning your financial future, it's essential to know what you have in order to make smart decisions.

While living within your means might not enable you to buy a bigger car, more expensive home or make larger investments right now, it can set you up for financial freedom later in life. This doesn't necessarily mean big changes have to occur in your current lifestyle, but understanding your finances can give you a better idea of what you will need down the road; as well as, how taxes and inflation can affect your income and expenses.

✓ **The only way to understand your money is to see everything in writing.** That's why we have created Your Personal Money Diary.

✓ **Your Personal Money Diary will track your expenses, debt, and even your income.** It will allow you to break down what you spend versus what you make and truly understand where your money is going.

✓ **Mapping out your yearly expenses, debt, and income can also assist you with prioritizing.** Maybe it's within your means to increase contributions toward retirement investments, or maybe it's in your best interest to focus on paying off loans first and then tackling savings. Your Personal Money Diary will offer inspiration and guidance every step of the way.

✓ **Organizing and understanding your finances can truly offer relief, peace of mind and excitement as you look towards the future.** Your Personal Money Diary will guide you through the process of calculating your yearly net income, fixed and flexible expenses, goals and net worth. Taking control of your financial past and present can liberate your financial future.

Crystal Moradi
Senior Vice President
PLJ Advisors

Personal Money Trainer

MOTIVATION STATION

Need a little inspiration to keep on track with your financial goals? Tape a photo, drawing, or anything that inspires you. Whether it's your children, grandchildren or the timeshare in Palm Beach, having a visual reminder in Your Personal Money Diary will help you.

MY GOALS

Planning for your financial future doesn't mean that you can't include fun events like vacations. It simply means that you have to put everything into perspective. It's a praiseworthy trait to have goals in mind, but you need to rationally consider short and long-term goals. Running off to the Caribbean this year sounds magnificent, but how will this affect paying your mortgage on time or saving for retirement? Listing your goals can help you make the best decisions, so you can achieve these objectives in a timely manner.

RESIST TEMPTATION Make a list when you go shopping. Just because something is on sale doesn't mean that it's a wise purchase. You save more by not buying something you don't need.

MONEY TIP

DID YOU KNOW?
Many television and internet service providers offer bundled services, allowing you discounts on internet, telephone, and cable packages. Check with the available providers in your area to see how you can save money on those services.

MY GOALS

"Goals are dreams with deadlines."
~ Diana Scharf Hunt

WHAT I WOULD LIKE TO ACCOMPLISH	DATE (OF COMPLETION)	HOW	AMOUNT (OF MONEY NEEDED)
1.			
2.			
3.			
4.			
5.			
6.			

MY YEARLY NET INCOME

Understanding your yearly net income can empower you to take control of your spending, so you can save responsibly. It can also help you achieve your dreams and the things you desire in the future.

Are you finding it a challenge to pay your fixed expenses on a regular basis? Then maybe you don't have enough money coming in to pay all your flexible expenses. Calculating your salaries and wages, as well as bonuses, interest from investments, and other sources of income can prevent you from going into debt. The key to being debt free is spending within your means and managing your annual income wisely. This is only possible if you determine your financial ceiling.

REWARD YOURSELF Sign up for every free customer rewards program you can. Create a separate email account for these mailings, collect reward cards and then check that account for additional coupons whenever you're ready to shop. **MONEY TIP**

DID YOU KNOW?
Some rewards programs are partnered with other merchants to offer benefits to customers from both ends. Check with your rewards clubs to see if you can get additional discounts on affiliate services.

MY YEARLY NET INCOME

INCOME	AMOUNT
Salaries & Wages	
Bonuses / Commissions	
Real Estate Income	
Interest / Dividends From Investment	
Income Tax Refunds	
Alimony / Child Support	
Other	
Other	
Other	
Other	
Other	
TOTAL:	

MONEY TIP

SAY BYE BYE TO BAD HABITS The Personal Money Trainer wants you to be healthy. Giving up expensive habits like cigarettes and alcohol prevents money from flowing away from you with nothing in return. Dig deep. Summon your willpower and work hard to kick these habits. You'll keep money in your pocket where it belongs.

NOTES

_____

_____

_____

_____

MY NET WORTH

In order to figure out your net worth, you need to identify your assets and your debt. You can use the figure representing what you own and deduct what you owe to determine your net worth (Assets - Liabilities = Net Worth). Because there are so many types of assets (e.g., cash, securities, real estate, etc.) and liabilities (e.g., current bills and various loans), it's beneficial to outline them and ensure that everything is included for an accurate value of your net worth.

INSTANT ACTION If a bill arrives in the mail, whether it's a utility bill, credit card bill or insurance, pay it off immediately! Once all the debts are taken care of at the beginning of the month, you have more freedom to spend on the things you want.

MONEY TIP

DID YOU KNOW?
Automatic Bill Pay, while convenient, can be detrimental to your spending habits. When you don't see where your money goes, you may forget that you've spent it. Paying bills manually allows you to see the value of your spending.

MY NET WORTH

ASSETS	AMOUNT
CASH	
Savings Account	
Checking Account	
Business Account	
Money Market Account	
Foreign Currency	
Other	
INVESTMENTS	
Government Bonds	
Other Bonds	
International Investments	
Stocks (Domestics / Foreign)	
CD's	
REAL ESTATE	
Domestic	
International	
MISC.	
Vehicles	
Precious Metals	
Luxury Collectibles	
Furniture	
Electronics	
Tools / Machinery	
INSURANCE	
Cash Settlements	
TOTAL:	

LIABILITIES	AMOUNT
LOAN	
Home	
Investment Property	
Car	
Education	
Credit Cards	
Tax	
CURRENT BILLS	
TAXES	
MISC.	
TOTAL:	

ASSETS	LIABILITIES	NET WORTH

TOTAL ASSETS - TOTAL LIABILITIES = NET WORTH

GET AUTOMATED Allot a certain amount of money each month to automatically be transferred into a savings account, so you're not tempted to spend it.

MONEY TIP

MY APPROXIMATE FIXED & FLEXIBLE EXPENSES

Expenses are items that are a cost to you. There are two types: fixed and flexible expenses. Fixed expenses are those that typically stay the same over periods of time and only fluctuate slightly if an adjustment occurs. This would include monthly rent or mortgage, car payments, property taxes, utilities and insurance premiums.

Flexible expenses are the costs that can be adjusted and sometimes even eliminated from your budget. Examples of these would be luxuries, such as dining out, clothing and other personal items. When determining what falls under which expense, ask yourself whether it's something you need versus something you want.

Calculating your fixed expenses can help you figure out where you could be saving money. Although you can't change your fixed costs, you can put restrictions and limits on the flexible costs. This will enable you to save and reduce your spending in certain areas such as entertainment, food (eating out), recreation and gifts. Are you ready to start decreasing those flexible expenses?

DID YOU KNOW?
A $5100 balance with an interest rate at 14.9% will cost you $760 a year in interest payments alone. Think about what you could do with $760 if you didn't have to pay it to the credit card company.

MY APPROXIMATE FIXED & FLEXIBLE EXPENSES

EXPENSES	MONTHLY	YEARLY
HOUSING		
Rent / Mortgage (Principal, Interest, Taxes)		
Home Association Fees		
Parking Garage or Space Rentals		
Electricity		
Gas		
Home Telephone		
Mobile Telephone		
Internet		
Home Improvement		
Utilities (Water / Sewer / Trash)		
Other		
TRANSPORTATION		
Car Payment(s)		
Car Registration(s)		
Gas / Fuel		
Maintenance (Regular Oil Change / Service)		
Repairs		
Public Transportation		
Other		
DAILY LIVING		
Groceries		
Dining / Eating Out		
Clothing / Shoes		
Cleaning Services (Dry Cleaning)		
Housekeeping		
Salon / Barber		
Other		
INSURANCE		
Life Insurance		
Health Insurance		
Dental Insurance		
Car Insurance		
Home Insurance		
MISC.		

MY APPROXIMATE FIXED & FLEXIBLE EXPENSES

EXPENSES	MONTHLY	YEARLY
HEALTH cont.		
Emergency		
Medicine / Drugs		
Other		
EDUCATION		
Tuition Fees		
Books		
School Supplies		
Lunch		
Clothing / Uniforms		
After School Care		
Other Specialty Courses		
Other		
SAVINGS		
Emergency Fund		
Savings Account		
Retirement (401K, IRA)		
College Fund		
Investment(s)		
Other		
CHARITY / GIFTS		
Religious Donations		
Medical Donations		
School Donations		
Charitable Donations		
Other		
DEBITS		
Alimony / Child Support		
Student Loan		
Bank Loan(s)		
Credit Card 1		
Credit Card 2		
Federal Taxes		
State Taxes		
Other		
ENTERTAINMENT		
DVD / CD		
Movies / Theaters		
Rentals		
Concerts / Plays		
Toys / Video Games		
Electronics		
Books		

MY APPROXIMATE FIXED & FLEXIBLE EXPENSES

EXPENSES	MONTHLY	YEARLY
ENTERTAINMENT cont.		
Film / Photos		
Sporting Events		
Outdoor Recreation		
Other		
Other		
BUSINESS		
Office Supplies		
Office Equipment		
Restaurants		
Travel		
Gas / Fuel		
Mileage		
Other		
VACATION		
Travel		
Rental		
Lodging		
Food / Dining Out		
Entertainment		
Fun Activities		
Gifts		
Other		
Other		
HOBBY		
Supplies		
Collectible Objects		
Tools / Equipment		
Other		
Other		
SUBSCRIPTIONS		
Magazines		
Newspapers		
Internet		
TV / Cable / Satellite		
Gym / Health Club		
Other		
MISC.		

MY MONTHLY EXPENSE SHEET

How much money do you spend every month? If you want to know where all of your hard-earned cash goes every 30 days, you have to follow it. Closely monitoring your flow of cash is tedious, but it can change your spending habits for the better and positively alter your financial outlook. Identifying your fixed and flexible expenses is information that makes up a monthly expense sheet. Once you're aware of these costs, you will have the knowledge to divide your money wisely among these expenses. Without knowing your monthly costs, it's impossible to have an idea of your yearly living expenses. Developing a monthly expense sheet might seem overwhelming because there are many variables to track. Approaching this task in an organized way can ease any hesitation you may have.

LOOK AHEAD Don't let the mistakes of your past drag you down. Look ahead to the future. The choices you make now are the ones that truly matter. By working hard to break patterns and establish new behavior, you'll be able to stay on track and avoid any financial pitfalls.

MONEY TIP

MY MONTHLY EXPENSE SHEET

It makes life easier when you know what your expenses are each month. Why live with uncertainty? Not only do you have bills and loans to plan for, but you also have goals and dreams such as vacations, homeownership, and retirement. Instead of letting these moments pass you by, develop a monthly expense sheet so you can be proactive now. Even taking a small step toward saving or paying off debts, will get you closer to reaching your aspirations. After you have completed your monthly expense sheet, you can move on to calculating your yearly living expenses.

This part of the process is the easiest, because all you have to do is multiply one month's worth of expenses by 12 months. Then you have your finances planned out in advance, which will enable you to stay on the green path to success! Tracking your monthly expenses in a chart format is an efficient method that will save you time and headaches. Including sections in the chart for savings, life, house, upkeep, utilities, etc. will serve as reminders for you to include all costs associated with these categories. For example, under utilities, you would add the costs for your cell phone, Internet, cable television, trash services, landline phone, gas, electricity, water, and sewer services. Have your bills and receipts readily available before beginning this task

CELL PHONE SAVVY Go through your cell phone bill and look for services you don't use and get rid of them. Whether it's texting, web access or recurring fees, these charges add up each month. Call your cell phone company and ask to have those services eliminated.

MONEY TIP

MY MONTHLY EXPENSES CHART

CATEGORIES	AMOUNT BUDGETED	ACTUAL AMOUNT														
Days of the Month		1	2	3	4	5	6	7	8	9	10	11	12	13	14	15
SAVINGS																
Emergency Savings																
Regular Savings																
401K																
INSURANCE																
Life																
Health / Dental / Vision																
Car																
HOUSE																
Rent / Mortgage																
Home Improvements																
Utilities																
AUTO																
Gas / Fuel																
Maintenance / Repairs																
Public Transportation																
FOOD																
Groceries																
Dining Out / Eating Out																
CLOTHING																
Clothes / Shoes / Accs.																
EDUCATION																
Tuition																
School Supplies																
Books																
After School Care																
VACATION																
Travel																
Lodging																
Food / Dining Out																
Other																
MISC.																
TOTAL:																

"We don't have an eternity to realize our dreams – only the time we are here."
~Susan L. Taylor

CATEGORIES	ACTUAL AMOUNT																
	16	17	18	19	20	21	22	23	24	25	26	27	28	29	30	31	Totals
SAVINGS																	
Emergency Savings																	
Regular Savings																	
401K																	
INSURANCE																	
Life																	
Health / Dental / Vision																	
Car																	
HOUSE																	
Rent / Mortgage																	
Home Improvements																	
Utilities																	
AUTO																	
Gas / Fuel																	
Maintenance / Repairs																	
Public Transportation																	
FOOD																	
Groceries																	
Dining Out / Eating Out																	
CLOTHING																	
Clothes / Shoes / Accs.																	
EDUCATION																	
Tuition																	
School Supplies																	
Books																	
After School Care																	
VACATION																	
Travel																	
Lodging																	
Food / Dining Out																	
Other																	
MISC.																	
TOTAL:																	TOTAL:

MONTHLY INCOME	AMOUNT SPENT	+ / -

MONTHLY INCOME - AMOUNT SPENT = AMOUNT SAVED OR OVER BUDGET

MY MONTHLY EXPENSES CHART

CATEGORIES	AMOUNT BUDGETED	ACTUAL AMOUNT													
Days of the Month		1	2	3	4	5	6	7	8	9	10	11	12	13	14
SAVINGS															
Emergency Savings															
Regular Savings															
401K															
INSURANCE															
Life															
Health / Dental / Vision															
Car															
HOUSE															
Rent / Mortgage															
Home Improvements															
Utilities															
AUTO															
Gas / Fuel															
Maintenance / Repairs															
Public Transportation															
FOOD															
Groceries															
Dining Out / Eating Out															
CLOTHING															
Clothes / Shoes / Accs.															
EDUCATION															
Tuition															
School Supplies															
Books															
After School Care															
VACATION															
Travel															
Lodging															
Food / Dining Out															
Other															
MISC.															
TOTAL:															

"Keep your dreams alive. Understand to achieve anything requires faith and belief in yourself, vision, hard work, determination, and dedication. Remember all things are possible for those who believe." ~Gail Devers

CATEGORIES	ACTUAL AMOUNT														
	15	16	17	18	19	20	21	22	23	24	25	26	27	28	Totals
SAVINGS															
Emergency Savings															
Regular Savings															
401K															
INSURANCE															
Life															
Health / Dental / Vision															
Car															
HOUSE															
Rent / Mortgage															
Home Improvements															
Utilities															
AUTO															
Gas / Fuel															
Maintenance / Repairs															
Public Transportation															
FOOD															
Groceries															
Dining Out / Eating Out															
CLOTHING															
Clothes / Shoes / Accs.															
EDUCATION															
Tuition															
School Supplies															
Books															
After School Care															
VACATION															
Travel															
Lodging															
Food / Dining Out															
Other															
MISC.															
TOTAL:															TOTAL:

MONTHLY INCOME	AMOUNT SPENT	+ / -

MONTHLY INCOME - AMOUNT SPENT = AMOUNT SAVED OR OVER BUDGET

MY MONTHLY EXPENSES CHART

CATEGORIES	AMOUNT BUDGETED	ACTUAL AMOUNT														
Days of the Month		1	2	3	4	5	6	7	8	9	10	11	12	13	14	15
SAVINGS																
Emergency Savings																
Regular Savings																
401K																
INSURANCE																
Life																
Health / Dental / Vision																
Car																
HOUSE																
Rent / Mortgage																
Home Improvements																
Utilities																
AUTO																
Gas / Fuel																
Maintenance / Repairs																
Public Transportation																
FOOD																
Groceries																
Dining Out / Eating Out																
CLOTHING																
Clothes / Shoes / Accs.																
EDUCATION																
Tuition																
School Supplies																
Books																
After School Care																
VACATION																
Travel																
Lodging																
Food / Dining Out																
Other																
MISC.																
TOTAL:																

"The road to success is always under construction." ~Lily Tomlin

CATEGORIES	ACTUAL AMOUNT																
	16	17	18	19	20	21	22	23	24	25	26	27	28	29	30	31	Totals
SAVINGS																	
Emergency Savings																	
Regular Savings																	
401K																	
INSURANCE																	
Life																	
Health / Dental / Vision																	
Car																	
HOUSE																	
Rent / Mortgage																	
Home Improvements																	
Utilities																	
AUTO																	
Gas / Fuel																	
Maintenance / Repairs																	
Public Transportation																	
FOOD																	
Groceries																	
Dining Out / Eating Out																	
CLOTHING																	
Clothes / Shoes / Accs.																	
EDUCATION																	
Tuition																	
School Supplies																	
Books																	
After School Care																	
VACATION																	
Travel																	
Lodging																	
Food / Dining Out																	
Other																	
MISC.																	
TOTAL:																	TOTAL:

MONTHLY INCOME	AMOUNT SPENT	+ / -

MONTHLY INCOME - AMOUNT SPENT = AMOUNT SAVED OR OVER BUDGET

MY MONTHLY EXPENSES CHART

CATEGORIES	AMOUNT BUDGETED	ACTUAL AMOUNT														
Days of the Month		1	2	3	4	5	6	7	8	9	10	11	12	13	14	15
SAVINGS																
Emergency Savings																
Regular Savings																
401K																
INSURANCE																
Life																
Health / Dental / Vision																
Car																
HOUSE																
Rent / Mortgage																
Home Improvements																
Utilities																
AUTO																
Gas / Fuel																
Maintenance / Repairs																
Public Transportation																
FOOD																
Groceries																
Dining Out / Eating Out																
CLOTHING																
Clothes / Shoes / Accs.																
EDUCATION																
Tuition																
School Supplies																
Books																
After School Care																
VACATION																
Travel																
Lodging																
Food / Dining Out																
Other																
MISC.																
TOTAL:																

"Courage doesn't always roar. Sometimes courage is the quiet voice at the end of the day saying, 'I will try again tomorrow.'" ~ Mary Anne Radmacher

CATEGORIES	ACTUAL AMOUNT															
	16	17	18	19	20	21	22	23	24	25	26	27	28	29	30	*Totals*
SAVINGS																
Emergency Savings																
Regular Savings																
401K																
INSURANCE																
Life																
Health / Dental / Vision																
Car																
HOUSE																
Rent / Mortgage																
Home Improvements																
Utilities																
AUTO																
Gas / Fuel																
Maintenance / Repairs																
Public Transportation																
FOOD																
Groceries																
Dining Out / Eating Out																
CLOTHING																
Clothes / Shoes / Accs.																
EDUCATION																
Tuition																
School Supplies																
Books																
After School Care																
VACATION																
Travel																
Lodging																
Food / Dining Out																
Other																
MISC.																
TOTAL:																TOTAL:

MONTHLY INCOME	AMOUNT SPENT	+ / -

MONTHLY INCOME - AMOUNT SPENT = AMOUNT SAVED OR OVER BUDGET

MY MONTHLY EXPENSES CHART

CATEGORIES	AMOUNT BUDGETED	ACTUAL AMOUNT														
Days of the Month		1	2	3	4	5	6	7	8	9	10	11	12	13	14	15
SAVINGS																
Emergency Savings																
Regular Savings																
401K																
INSURANCE																
Life																
Health / Dental / Vision																
Car																
HOUSE																
Rent / Mortgage																
Home Improvements																
Utilities																
AUTO																
Gas / Fuel																
Maintenance / Repairs																
Public Transportation																
FOOD																
Groceries																
Dining Out / Eating Out																
CLOTHING																
Clothes / Shoes / Accs.																
EDUCATION																
Tuition																
School Supplies																
Books																
After School Care																
VACATION																
Travel																
Lodging																
Food / Dining Out																
Other																
MISC.																
TOTAL:																

"Love life, engage in it, give it all you've got. Love it with a passion, because life truly does give back, many times over, what you put into it." ~Maya Angelou

CATEGORIES	ACTUAL AMOUNT																
	16	17	18	19	20	21	22	23	24	25	26	27	28	29	30	31	Totals
SAVINGS																	
Emergency Savings																	
Regular Savings																	
401K																	
INSURANCE																	
Life																	
Health / Dental / Vision																	
Car																	
HOUSE																	
Rent / Mortgage																	
Home Improvements																	
Utilities																	
AUTO																	
Gas / Fuel																	
Maintenance / Repairs																	
Public Transportation																	
FOOD																	
Groceries																	
Dining Out / Eating Out																	
CLOTHING																	
Clothes / Shoes / Accs.																	
EDUCATION																	
Tuition																	
School Supplies																	
Books																	
After School Care																	
VACATION																	
Travel																	
Lodging																	
Food / Dining Out																	
Other																	
MISC.																	
TOTAL:																	TOTAL:

MONTHLY INCOME	AMOUNT SPENT	+ / -
MONTHLY INCOME - AMOUNT SPENT = AMOUNT SAVED OR OVER BUDGET		

MY MONTHLY EXPENSES CHART

CATEGORIES	AMOUNT BUDGETED	ACTUAL AMOUNT														
Days of the Month		1	2	3	4	5	6	7	8	9	10	11	12	13	14	15
SAVINGS																
Emergency Savings																
Regular Savings																
401K																
INSURANCE																
Life																
Health / Dental / Vision																
Car																
HOUSE																
Rent / Mortgage																
Home Improvements																
Utilities																
AUTO																
Gas / Fuel																
Maintenance / Repairs																
Public Transportation																
FOOD																
Groceries																
Dining Out / Eating Out																
CLOTHING																
Clothes / Shoes / Accs.																
EDUCATION																
Tuition																
School Supplies																
Books																
After School Care																
VACATION																
Travel																
Lodging																
Food / Dining Out																
Other																
MISC.																
TOTAL:																

"You may be disappointed if you fail, but you are doomed if you don't try."
~Beverly Sills

JUNE _____

CATEGORIES	ACTUAL AMOUNT															
	16	17	18	19	20	21	22	23	24	25	26	27	28	29	30	Totals
SAVINGS																
Emergency Savings																
Regular Savings																
401K																
INSURANCE																
Life																
Health / Dental / Vision																
Car																
HOUSE																
Rent / Mortgage																
Home Improvements																
Utilities																
AUTO																
Gas / Fuel																
Maintenance / Repairs																
Public Transportation																
FOOD																
Groceries																
Dining Out / Eating Out																
CLOTHING																
Clothes / Shoes / Accs.																
EDUCATION																
Tuition																
School Supplies																
Books																
After School Care																
VACATION																
Travel																
Lodging																
Food / Dining Out																
Other																
MISC.																
TOTAL:																TOTAL:

MONTHLY INCOME	AMOUNT SPENT	+ / -

MONTHLY INCOME - AMOUNT SPENT = AMOUNT SAVED OR OVER BUDGET

MY MONTHLY EXPENSES CHART

CATEGORIES	AMOUNT BUDGETED	ACTUAL AMOUNT														
Days of the Month		1	2	3	4	5	6	7	8	9	10	11	12	13	14	15
SAVINGS																
Emergency Savings																
Regular Savings																
401K																
INSURANCE																
Life																
Health / Dental / Vision																
Car																
HOUSE																
Rent / Mortgage																
Home Improvements																
Utilities																
AUTO																
Gas / Fuel																
Maintenance / Repairs																
Public Transportation																
FOOD																
Groceries																
Dining Out / Eating Out																
CLOTHING																
Clothes / Shoes / Accs.																
EDUCATION																
Tuition																
School Supplies																
Books																
After School Care																
VACATION																
Travel																
Lodging																
Food / Dining Out																
Other																
MISC.																
TOTAL:																

"I'm not afraid of storms, for I'm learning to sail my ship." ~Louisa May Alcott

CATEGORIES	ACTUAL AMOUNT																
	16	17	18	19	20	21	22	23	24	25	26	27	28	29	30	31	*Totals*
SAVINGS																	
Emergency Savings																	
Regular Savings																	
401K																	
INSURANCE																	
Life																	
Health / Dental / Vision																	
Car																	
HOUSE																	
Rent / Mortgage																	
Home Improvements																	
Utilities																	
AUTO																	
Gas / Fuel																	
Maintenance / Repairs																	
Public Transportation																	
FOOD																	
Groceries																	
Dining Out / Eating Out																	
CLOTHING																	
Clothes / Shoes / Accs.																	
EDUCATION																	
Tuition																	
School Supplies																	
Books																	
After School Care																	
VACATION																	
Travel																	
Lodging																	
Food / Dining Out																	
Other																	
MISC.																	
TOTAL:																	**TOTAL:**

MONTHLY INCOME	AMOUNT SPENT	+ / -

MONTHLY INCOME - AMOUNT SPENT = AMOUNT SAVED OR OVER BUDGET

MY MONTHLY EXPENSES CHART

CATEGORIES	AMOUNT BUDGETED	ACTUAL AMOUNT														
Days of the Month		1	2	3	4	5	6	7	8	9	10	11	12	13	14	15
SAVINGS																
Emergency Savings																
Regular Savings																
401K																
INSURANCE																
Life																
Health / Dental / Vision																
Car																
HOUSE																
Rent / Mortgage																
Home Improvements																
Utilities																
AUTO																
Gas / Fuel																
Maintenance / Repairs																
Public Transportation																
FOOD																
Groceries																
Dining Out / Eating Out																
CLOTHING																
Clothes / Shoes / Accs.																
EDUCATION																
Tuition																
School Supplies																
Books																
After School Care																
VACATION																
Travel																
Lodging																
Food / Dining Out																
Other																
MISC.																
TOTAL:																

"Just don't give up trying to do what you really want to do. Where there is love and inspiration, I don't think you can go wrong." ~Ella Fitzgerald

CATEGORIES	ACTUAL AMOUNT																
	16	17	18	19	20	21	22	23	24	25	26	27	28	29	30	31	*Totals*
SAVINGS																	
Emergency Savings																	
Regular Savings																	
401K																	
INSURANCE																	
Life																	
Health / Dental / Vision																	
Car																	
HOUSE																	
Rent / Mortgage																	
Home Improvements																	
Utilities																	
AUTO																	
Gas / Fuel																	
Maintenance / Repairs																	
Public Transportation																	
FOOD																	
Groceries																	
Dining Out / Eating Out																	
CLOTHING																	
Clothes / Shoes / Accs.																	
EDUCATION																	
Tuition																	
School Supplies																	
Books																	
After School Care																	
VACATION																	
Travel																	
Lodging																	
Food / Dining Out																	
Other																	
MISC.																	
TOTAL:																	TOTAL:

MONTHLY INCOME	AMOUNT SPENT	+ / -

MONTHLY INCOME - AMOUNT SPENT = AMOUNT SAVED OR OVER BUDGET

MY MONTHLY EXPENSES CHART

CATEGORIES	AMOUNT BUDGETED	ACTUAL AMOUNT														
Days of the Month		1	2	3	4	5	6	7	8	9	10	11	12	13	14	15
SAVINGS																
Emergency Savings																
Regular Savings																
401K																
INSURANCE																
Life																
Health / Dental / Vision																
Car																
HOUSE																
Rent / Mortgage																
Home Improvements																
Utilities																
AUTO																
Gas / Fuel																
Maintenance / Repairs																
Public Transportation																
FOOD																
Groceries																
Dining Out / Eating Out																
CLOTHING																
Clothes / Shoes / Accs.																
EDUCATION																
Tuition																
School Supplies																
Books																
After School Care																
VACATION																
Travel																
Lodging																
Food / Dining Out																
Other																
MISC.																
TOTAL:																

"The minute you alter your perception of yourself and your future, both you and your future begin to change." ~Marilee Zdenek

SEPTEMBER _____

CATEGORIES	ACTUAL AMOUNT															
	16	17	18	19	20	21	22	23	24	25	26	27	28	29	30	Totals
SAVINGS																
Emergency Savings																
Regular Savings																
401K																
INSURANCE																
Life																
Health / Dental / Vision																
Car																
HOUSE																
Rent / Mortgage																
Home Improvements																
Utilities																
AUTO																
Gas / Fuel																
Maintenance / Repairs																
Public Transportation																
FOOD																
Groceries																
Dining Out / Eating Out																
CLOTHING																
Clothes / Shoes / Accs.																
EDUCATION																
Tuition																
School Supplies																
Books																
After School Care																
VACATION																
Travel																
Lodging																
Food / Dining Out																
Other																
MISC.																
TOTAL:																TOTAL:

MONTHLY INCOME	AMOUNT SPENT	+ / -

MONTHLY INCOME - AMOUNT SPENT = AMOUNT SAVED OR OVER BUDGET

MY MONTHLY EXPENSES CHART

CATEGORIES	AMOUNT BUDGETED	ACTUAL AMOUNT														
Days of the Month		1	2	3	4	5	6	7	8	9	10	11	12	13	14	15
SAVINGS																
Emergency Savings																
Regular Savings																
401K																
INSURANCE																
Life																
Health / Dental / Vision																
Car																
HOUSE																
Rent / Mortgage																
Home Improvements																
Utilities																
AUTO																
Gas / Fuel																
Maintenance / Repairs																
Public Transportation																
FOOD																
Groceries																
Dining Out / Eating Out																
CLOTHING																
Clothes / Shoes / Accs.																
EDUCATION																
Tuition																
School Supplies																
Books																
After School Care																
VACATION																
Travel																
Lodging																
Food / Dining Out																
Other																
MISC.																
TOTAL:																

"You are never too old to set another goal or to dream a new dream." ~C.S. Lewis

CATEGORIES	ACTUAL AMOUNT																
	16	17	18	19	20	21	22	23	24	25	26	27	28	29	30	31	Totals
SAVINGS																	
Emergency Savings																	
Regular Savings																	
401K																	
INSURANCE																	
Life																	
Health / Dental / Vision																	
Car																	
HOUSE																	
Rent / Mortgage																	
Home Improvements																	
Utilities																	
AUTO																	
Gas / Fuel																	
Maintenance / Repairs																	
Public Transportation																	
FOOD																	
Groceries																	
Dining Out / Eating Out																	
CLOTHING																	
Clothes / Shoes / Accs.																	
EDUCATION																	
Tuition																	
School Supplies																	
Books																	
After School Care																	
VACATION																	
Travel																	
Lodging																	
Food / Dining Out																	
Other																	
MISC.																	
TOTAL:																	TOTAL:

MONTHLY INCOME	AMOUNT SPENT	+ / -

MONTHLY INCOME - AMOUNT SPENT = AMOUNT SAVED OR OVER BUDGET

MY MONTHLY EXPENSES CHART

CATEGORIES	AMOUNT BUDGETED	ACTUAL AMOUNT														
Days of the Month		1	2	3	4	5	6	7	8	9	10	11	12	13	14	15
SAVINGS																
Emergency Savings																
Regular Savings																
401K																
INSURANCE																
Life																
Health / Dental / Vision																
Car																
HOUSE																
Rent / Mortgage																
Home Improvements																
Utilities																
AUTO																
Gas / Fuel																
Maintenance / Repairs																
Public Transportation																
FOOD																
Groceries																
Dining Out / Eating Out																
CLOTHING																
Clothes / Shoes / Accs.																
EDUCATION																
Tuition																
School Supplies																
Books																
After School Care																
VACATION																
Travel																
Lodging																
Food / Dining Out																
Other																
MISC.																
TOTAL:																

"Reach high, for stars lie hidden in your soul. Dream deep, for every dream precedes the goal." ~Pamela Vaull Starr

CATEGORIES	ACTUAL AMOUNT															
	16	17	18	19	20	21	22	23	24	25	26	27	28	29	30	*Totals*
SAVINGS																
Emergency Savings																
Regular Savings																
401K																
INSURANCE																
Life																
Health / Dental / Vision																
Car																
HOUSE																
Rent / Mortgage																
Home Improvements																
Utilities																
AUTO																
Gas / Fuel																
Maintenance / Repairs																
Public Transportation																
FOOD																
Groceries																
Dining Out / Eating Out																
CLOTHING																
Clothes / Shoes / Accs.																
EDUCATION																
Tuition																
School Supplies																
Books																
After School Care																
VACATION																
Travel																
Lodging																
Food / Dining Out																
Other																
MISC.																
TOTAL:																TOTAL:

MONTHLY INCOME	AMOUNT SPENT	+ / -

MONTHLY INCOME - AMOUNT SPENT = AMOUNT SAVED OR OVER BUDGET

MY MONTHLY EXPENSES CHART

CATEGORIES	AMOUNT BUDGETED	ACTUAL AMOUNT														
Days of the Month		1	2	3	4	5	6	7	8	9	10	11	12	13	14	15
SAVINGS																
Emergency Savings																
Regular Savings																
401K																
INSURANCE																
Life																
Health / Dental / Vision																
Car																
HOUSE																
Rent / Mortgage																
Home Improvements																
Utilities																
AUTO																
Gas / Fuel																
Maintenance / Repairs																
Public Transportation																
FOOD																
Groceries																
Dining Out / Eating Out																
CLOTHING																
Clothes / Shoes / Accs.																
EDUCATION																
Tuition																
School Supplies																
Books																
After School Care																
VACATION																
Travel																
Lodging																
Food / Dining Out																
Other																
MISC.																
TOTAL:																

"Be thankful for what you have; you'll end up having more. If you concentrate on what you don't have, you will never, ever have enough." ~Oprah Winfrey

CATEGORIES	ACTUAL AMOUNT																
	16	17	18	19	20	21	22	23	24	25	26	27	28	29	30	31	Totals
SAVINGS																	
Emergency Savings																	
Regular Savings																	
401K																	
INSURANCE																	
Life																	
Health / Dental / Vision																	
Car																	
HOUSE																	
Rent / Mortgage																	
Home Improvements																	
Utilities																	
AUTO																	
Gas / Fuel																	
Maintenance / Repairs																	
Public Transportation																	
FOOD																	
Groceries																	
Dining Out / Eating Out																	
CLOTHING																	
Clothes / Shoes / Accs.																	
EDUCATION																	
Tuition																	
School Supplies																	
Books																	
After School Care																	
VACATION																	
Travel																	
Lodging																	
Food / Dining Out																	
Other																	
MISC.																	
TOTAL:																	TOTAL:

MONTHLY INCOME	AMOUNT SPENT	+ / -

MONTHLY INCOME - AMOUNT SPENT = AMOUNT SAVED OR OVER BUDGET

MY ACTUAL YEARLY EXPENSES

Now that you know what you've spent each month, you can see what your actual expenses are for the entire year. Did you come up short on your goals, meet them or surpass them? Your Yearly Expense Chart will not only help you see the big financial picture but it can also assist you when tax time rolls around.

THIRTY SECOND RULE Whenever you're shopping and you find an item you want to purchase, stop for thirty seconds, and ask yourself why you're buying it, and whether you actually need it. If you can't find a good answer, put the item back. This will keep you from making impulse buys on a regular basis.

MONEY TIP

DID YOU KNOW?
Impulse purchases represent almost 40% of all money spent on ecommerce sites. People are more drawn to impulse buying based on the design elements of the site, not the price. Don't let the design trick you into buying something that you don't need or for a higher price than you would rather pay.

MY ACTUAL YEARLY EXPENSES

EXPENSES	ACTUAL AMOUNT											
	JAN	FEB	MAR	APR	MAY	JUN	JUL	AUG	SEP	OCT	NOV	DEC
HOUSE												
Rent / Mortgage												
Home Improvements												
Water / Sewer / Trash												
Home / Cell Phone												
Internet												
TV / Cable / Satellite												
Furnishings												
Other												
AUTOMOBILE												
Car Payments												
Maintenance / Repairs												
Gas / Fuel												
Other												
INSURANCE												
Life												
Medical / Dental / Vision												
House												
Car												
FOOD												
Groceries												
Dining Out / Eating Out												
EDUCATION												
Tuition Fees												
School Supplies / Books												
After School Care												
Other												
PERSONAL												
Grooming / Salon												
Clothing / Shoes												
Other												
FUN												
Entertainment / Toys												
Recreation												
Gifts												
TOTALS:												

YEARLY INCOME	YEARLY EXPENDITURE	+ / -

YEARLY INCOME - YEARLY EXPENDITURE = AMOUNT SAVED OR OVER BUDGET

THIRTY DAY MONEY FAST

When you're considering making an unnecessary purchase (i.e. a big ticket item, flat screen, iPad, etc.), wait thirty days, and then ask yourself if you still want that item. You may find that the urge to buy has passed, and you'll have saved money by simply waiting. We've included a "thirty day list" where you can write down the item and the day you'll reconsider this purchase. Chances are, at the end of thirty days, you'll realize just how unnecessary this purchase is.

CARDIO CARDS Play hide and seek with your credit cards. Take your credit cards and put them in a safe place in your home, not in your wallet where it's easy to use them. If you're worried about "emergencies," keep a small amount of cash hidden in your wallet for these situations. Don't keep cards on you until you have the willpower to not use it even when you're sorely tempted.

MONEY TIP

DID YOU KNOW?
In 2006, the credit card industry took $55 Billion in credit card fees and $90 Billion in finance charges. Protect yourself by not having a revolving credit line and not opening too many credit card accounts.

THIRTY DAY MONEY FAST

MY DESIRED PURCHASES

1.	
2.	
3.	
4.	
5.	
6.	
7.	
8.	
9.	
10.	
11.	
12.	
13.	
14.	
15.	
16.	
17.	
18.	
19.	
20.	
21.	
22.	
23.	
24.	
25.	
26.	
27.	
28.	
29.	
30.	

TOP 10 EVERYDAY SAVINGS TIPS

1. Allot a certain amount of money each month to automatically be put into a savings account, so you're not as tempted to spend more money.

2. Keep a record of every dollar you spend, so you have a better idea where you are overspending. Once you identify these areas, you can figure out ways to save more.

3. Avoid impulse shopping by having a list of the things you need when you go out shopping. Just because something is on sale, doesn't mean it's a wise purchase. You save more by not buying what you don't need.

4. Carefully watch how you use your credit cards. It's always best to first try using cash or debit (especially on smaller items). That way you will only be spending the money you have. Try using credit cards for emergency or larger items only.

5. Lower your monthly food costs by looking for generic brand items, items that are on sale, and items in bulk. Also, try minimizing the amount of times you eat-out. Bring lunches to work instead of buying them.

6. Set aside a limited budget for entertainment. Save money by renting movies, going to a matinee, checking out books and magazines from the library, and by attending free events at local parks or museums.

7. Save money by taking public transportation, and save money on gas by maintaining your vehicle. Simple things such as having your engine tuned regularly will help you get more mileage out of each tank of gas.

8. Anytime a bill comes in, whether it is a credit card bill, insurance bill, electricity bill, etc., make sure to pay it off immediately! After all the debts are taken care of at the beginning of the month, you have more freedom in how you spend the rest of the money.

9. When you're booking flights for your next trip, look around to see if there are any special deals for weekdays or weekends. Try seeing if booking your flight for a different date will help you cut down your costs.

10. Next time your doctor calls in a prescription, check to see if there's a generic brand of your medication.

MONEY TIP

SEE YOUR GOAL Create a visual reminder of your debt and goals. KeepYOUR PERSONAL MONEY DIARY in a place where you'll see it often, and keep filling it in regularly. It will keep your eyes on the prize.

TIPS FOR THE HOLIDAY BUDGETER

✓ **BE AN EARLY BIRD**

Watch for sales all year round and buy gifts throughout the year. Many stores have after-holiday mark downs where you can stock up on gifts for the following year. Gift bags, gift wrap, tissue paper, and ribbon also get marked down after the holidays. You can look for solid colors to use throughout the year for birthday and other non-holiday gifts. Buying in advance also spreads the money you will be spending out over a longer period of time, so you don't get hit with a bunch of expenses at the end of the year.

✓ **WATCH THE NUMBERS**

Keep an eye out for sales. Set Google alerts for your favorite stores or giveaways. Check shopping sites that offer sample sales for great gift ideas at up to 50-75 percent discounts.

✓ **BE FRUGAL**

In addition to looking out for sales, you can plan some frugal gift ideas. Visit a dollar store and pick up some picture frames or mugs. You can fill these with pictures of your kids, or yourself, depending on who you intend to give them to. Fill mugs with homemade treats or hot chocolate packets. You can wrap them in colorful paper and ribbon for an inexpensive but thoughtful gift.

DID YOU KNOW?

Cyber Monday, which falls on the Monday after Thanksgiving, is the day that online retailers provide deep discounts for holiday shopping. You can get the same discount as Black Friday without having to wait in line at 4AM or even leaving the comfort of your home.

HOLIDAY GIFT LIST

NAME	GIFT IDEA, STORES, SALE PRICES	BUDGET	ACTUAL COST
	TOTALS:		

HOLIDAY BUDGETER

The holidays are a time where many people spend a ton of money and run up their credit card balances. If you're working towards a financial goal, holidays can often derail progress. That's why we've included our Holiday Budgeter.

HOLIDAY EXPENSES	BUDGETED COSTS	ACTUAL COSTS
TOTALS:		

DID YOU KNOW?
Majority of people who are given gift cards say that they typically spend more than the value of the card when they use the card for a purchase. As a budgeting tip, awareness of that fact may help you avoid over-spending.

PANTRY PATROL

Are you looking for ways to cut back? Your pantry may be the easiest place to start. Below, we offer a number of helpful tips to lower your food bill and bolster your bank account.

- ✓ Reduce the number of days you eat out.
- ✓ Skip the lattes and make your own at home. Buying a latte every day can total up to $1,200 per year!
- ✓ Eat oatmeal or toast for breakfast.
- ✓ Cook from staples rather than mixes and cans.
- ✓ Learn to cook.
- ✓ Eat fruit for snacks.
- ✓ Eat beans and legumes instead of meat.
- ✓ Invest some time into food preparation and preserving. You'd be surprised how much you can save per hour.
- ✓ Don't give your children the choice to be too picky.
- ✓ Buy staples in the largest size bag you can find and make space for it.
- ✓ Don't let food go bad in your fridge.
- ✓ Grow a garden.
- ✓ Shop in produce stores. They are cheaper, and there is less to tempt you.
- ✓ Don't shop hungry.
- ✓ Try using cheaper substitutes for items in a recipe.
- ✓ Don't buy name brand products.
- ✓ Try finding local ethnic markets.
- ✓ Try processing your own food. (Make your own yogurt, cheese, etc.)
- ✓ Save leftovers for lunch the next day.
- ✓ Pack your lunch rather than buying it.
- ✓ Get your partner on board.

THE MOST IMPORTANT MEAL OF THE DAY Eating a healthy breakfast fills you up with energy for the day and can decrease those urges to grab an unhealthy or expensive lunch.

MONEY TIP

SHOPPING LIST

Make Copies for Everyday Use!

Making a grocery list helps you avoid loading your cart with unnecessary purchases. We've included this helpful shopping list to track your expenses and any coupon savings you may find.

TO PURCHASE	PRICE	COUPON?	Notes
○		○	
○		○	
○		○	
○		○	
○		○	
○		○	
○		○	
○		○	
○		○	
○		○	
○		○	
○		○	
○		○	
○		○	
○		○	
○		○	
○		○	
○		○	
○		○	
○		○	
○		○	
○		○	
○		○	
○		○	
○		○	
○		○	
○		○	
○		○	
○		○	
○		○	
○		○	
○		○	
○		○	

TRAVEL TONE-UP

Even the savviest savers need a vacation. Whether you're a first-class-all-the-way or an all-about-the-budget kind of traveler, there's always savings to be had. Whether it's catching a new show, getting a massage or enjoying a five star dining experience, our travel tone-up will help you create a trip you and your pocketbook can both enjoy.

- ✓ Use reward points for airline tickets and hotel rooms.
- ✓ Visit top destinations in the off season.
- ✓ Stay with friends and relatives and offer your home in return.
- ✓ Check travel sites that offer discount rates.
- ✓ Consider renting an apartment or condo if staying in an area for an extended period of time.
- ✓ Eat your biggest meal at lunch when eating out.
- ✓ Ask for specials or deals when making travel arrangements.
- ✓ Travel light and avoid baggage charges.
- ✓ Park in the furthest extended stay parking lot at airports for the best daily fees.
- ✓ Check the web for discount coupons for rental cars, hotels, restaurants and attractions.
- ✓ Check your insurance coverage to see what coverage you have so you don't pay to duplicate on a rental car.
- ✓ Inquire about multiple day discounts on rental cars.
- ✓ Before you depart, check with your bank and find ATM's along your route to see where you can get cash without paying fees.
- ✓ Ask locals about good places to eat at reasonable prices.
- ✓ Use public transportation.
- ✓ Entertain yourself– check out free events in the areas you are visiting.
- ✓ Stop at visitors centers for discount coupons and advice on the must-see destinations.
- ✓ If you're a last minute traveler, check out discounts offered by cruise lines, hotels or airlines who want to fill vacancies.
- ✓ Purchase all-inclusive packages.

DID YOU KNOW?
Many destinations have online travel forums that offer tips on saving money on your travel expenses. Tap into a community of travel experts or locals who are willing to share how to get the best bang for your buck. However, be sure to check on a site's reputation before trusting tips.

TRAVEL BUDGETING CHECKLIST

Vacations are meant to be enjoyed, but understanding what you're spending will keep you from making any unnecessary detours. That's why we've provided you with this easy to follow checklist that will help keep you on track even when you're on the road.

BEFORE YOU GO	AMOUNT
Wardrobe Necessities (See Packing)	
Baggage	
Passports / Photos	
Medications / Innoculations	
Sunscreen, Aloe, Sunglasses, Hats	
Baby-sitters / Pet Sitters	
Cameras	

TRAVEL	AMOUNT
BY CAR:	
Gas / Oil	
Tolls / Tips	
Meals / Snacks / Souvenirs	
Other Transportation (Cabs, Subways, Buses, Etc.)	
BY PLANE:	
Airport Transportation (Taxi, Long-Term Parking, Etc.)	
Magazines, Snacks, Etc. (Round Trip)	

DESTINATION	AMOUNT
Room Rates (X's # of Nights) (Taxes Included)	
Breakfast (X's # of Days)	
Lunch (X's # of Days)	
Dinner (X's # of Days)	
Beer / Wine / Alcoholic Beverages	
Snacks	
Tips (X's # of Days)	
Phone / Internet / In-Room Movies	
Souvenirs / Postcards	
Activities (Scuba Diving, Horseback Riding, Tours, Etc.)	
Entertainment (Shows, Movies, Fair Admissions)	
Misc.	
TOTALS:	

ENERGY POW WOW

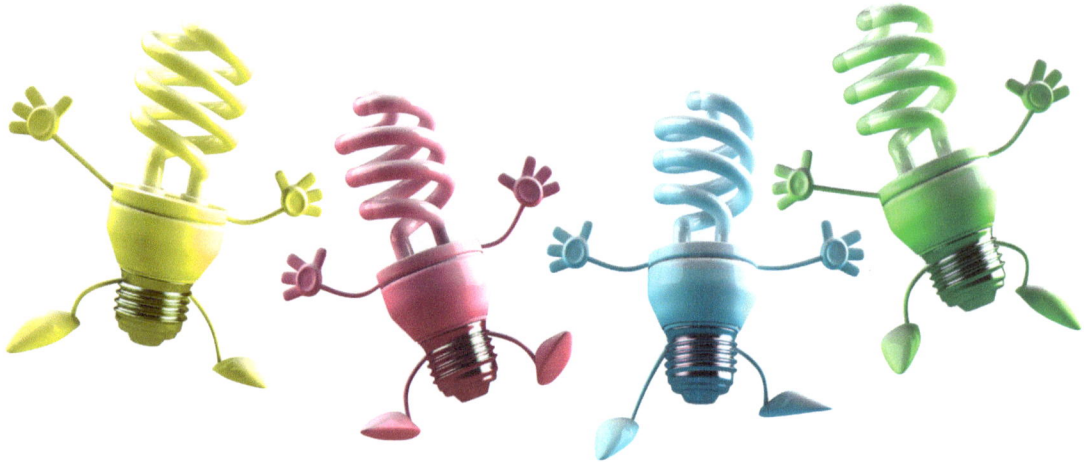

What would you say if you knew that you had hundreds, maybe even thousands of dollars in savings right under your nose? Your home, if you look closely, could be costing you a fortune. Luckily for you, going green can put extra money in your pocket. Reviewing your appliances and the daily energy usage in your home, can not only help you save those hard earned dollars, but can help you do your part for the planet. Here's your list of things to do in order to complete Your Personal Money Diary's Energy Pow Wow.

- ✓ Use energy-saving settings on refrigerators, dishwashers, washing machines, and clothes dryers.
- ✓ Review your standard (incandescent) light bulbs and learn whether or not you can replace them with compact fluorescents. Compact fluorescent lamps (CFLs) can save three-quarters of the electricity used by incandescent bulbs. The best targets are 60-100 watt bulbs used several hours a day.
- ✓ Check the age and condition of your major appliances, especially your refrigerator. It may be more cost effective to replace older appliances with a more energy-efficient model instead of waiting until it breaks down.
- ✓ Look for Energy Star labels when it's time to replace your heating or cooling system (or other appliances). They may cost you more but there will be savings in the long run.
- ✓ Clean or replace furnace, air-conditioner, and heat-pump filters.
- ✓ Properly maintain your heating and cooling systems and upgrade the equipment when needed.
- ✓ Review your utility bills. Separate electricity and fuel bills. Target the biggest bill for energy conservation remedies.
- ✓ Schedule an energy audit for more expert advice on your entire home.
- ✓ Don't let leaky windows cost you. Be sure to upgrade them with energy-efficient models or to boost their efficiency with weather stripping and storm windows.
- ✓ Go green outdoors. Planting shade trees and shrubs around your house, especially the west side, can significantly reduce air conditioning costs.
- ✓ Has your attic or crawlspace been inspected for insulation? Is there any? How much?
- ✓ Insulate ducts wherever they run through unheated areas.
- ✓ Install a clock thermostat to set your thermostat back automatically at night.
- ✓ Contact your local electric company for information about energy efficiency.
- ✓ Don't heat or cool when you're not home. Be sure to turn down the thermostat, especially when leaving your house and at night. You may want to consider installing a timer that automatically does it for you.
- ✓ Turn off the computer. You will conserve energy by turning off or using sleep mode for any computer not in use for two hours or more.

GETTING YOUR GREEN ON

Who knew saving money and doing your part for the planet was so easy? We've included these fun facts to get you started and help bring green to all areas of your life.

1. THE SCENT OF SAVINGS

Use all natural deodorant. You can find these at nearly any health food or natural living store. They last forever, have no harmful ingredients, and they come in recyclable packaging, so you're not clogging up those landfills.

2. JAVA REJUVENATION

Reusable coffee filters are a great way to get your caffeine fix without forking over a fortune.

3. BOUNTY BE GONE

Get rid of paper towels. Not an easy thing to do but using old t-shirts and rags and making sure you have plenty stored away can be just as easy (and cost effective).

4. BE A BAG LADY

Recycle your plastic bags. Despite the call to arms to rid stores of plastic, it still remains the popular choice. While the temptation may be to throw them out with the rest of the trash, we suggest finding other uses for them. You can use them to line small trash cans (one less item to buy), pick up after your dog in the park, or use it for packaging gifts. You can also look for affordable reusable bags and bring them with you when you shop.

5. H20 TO GO

Buy a water filter and install it in your kitchen. You can save thousands of dollars by not buying packages of bottled water. Also, purchase an inexpensive water bottle. They have plenty of uniquely designed ones, something you'll want to carry with you. It will also help avoid those impulse bottled water buys when you're not at home.

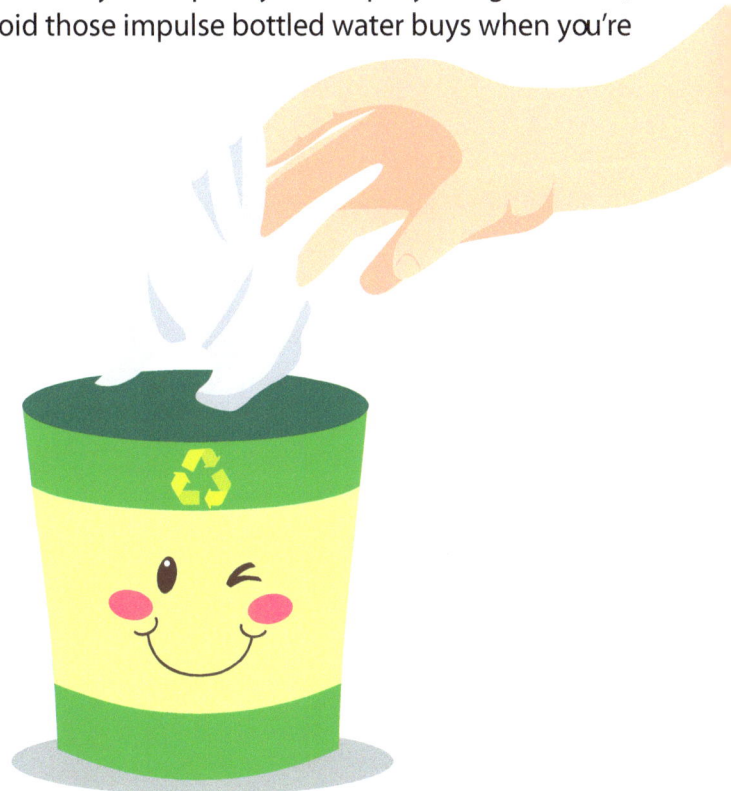

RUN FOR YOUR MONEY

CASH, CREDIT, DEBIT?

Do you ever consider your safest way to pay for purchases? With identity theft becoming one of the fastest growing crimes in the country, it's more important than ever to be aware - not just what you're buying but how.

According to the Javelin 2010 Identity Theft Report, 11.1 million adults were victims of identity theft in 2009. The total fraud amount was $54 billion. The average victim spent 21 hours and $373 out of pocket resolving the crime. We understand how busy you are, and the last thing we want is for you to have to spend countless hours and hard earned dollars reclaiming what's rightfully yours. Luckily for you, we've provided a list of suggestions on the safest methods of payments, so you can stay one step ahead of the crooks.

Not only that, but our list will help you understand how certain types of payment options take the power away from the consumer. The Credit Card Debit Challenge gives you, the consumer, the power and knowledge to understand the safest way to pay.

REMINDER: Inspect the ATM before using. With technology improving daily, criminal skimmers are becoming more advanced. If something seems off or not right about the ATM machine or card reader, don't use it. Even if this ATM is on bank property, it might have been compromised. Always be aware of your surroundings when using an ATM as well. You can never be too safe.

ONLINE SHOPPING

Use a credit card. For online purchases, DON'T use your debit card. Your debit card is linked directly to your checking account. This means that your checking account is vulnerable to thieves using your debit card number to clean out your account. In case of fraudulent use, your bank is likely under regulation to limit your liability, but you will still have to endure the hassle of getting your balance restored which might take some time. During that time, you may, experience other problems because the balance in your checking account is not what you expected, and scheduled payments are going through.

RUN FOR YOUR MONEY

RESTAURANTS

Upscale Dining

Use cash. Don't use a debit card. The same rules which apply here are mentioned under Online Purchases.

Fast Food Restaurants

Use a credit card • Use a debit card • Use cash. If you're paying at the register when you order, use your debit card or cash.

LARGE TICKET ITEMS

Use a credit card. Shopping for a new flat screen or home entertainment system? Most credit cards offer more consumer rights if there's an issue or dispute with the vendor. A debit card doesn't always offer this same protection. And if you already paid in cash, you don't have any leverage if you dispute the charges. Some credit cards also offer extended warrantees. And in some purchases, such as buying electronics or renting a car, some credit cards also offer additional property insurance to cover the item.

DEPOSITS

Use a credit card. This provides the store with its security deposit, and you still have access to all of the money in your bank account. If you were to use cash or debit, you may have a dispute and become unable to get the deposit money back.

RECURRING PAYMENTS

Use a credit card. Imagine the hassle that might be involved with trying to stop a membership payment for something like a dormant health club membership. Now imagine the charges aren't going onto your credit card, but instead coming right out of your bank account.

FUTURE TRAVEL PURCHASES

Use a credit card. If you use your debit card, you will be debited almost immediately, even for travel or delivery in the future. So if you're purchasing travel tickets you won't receive or use for six months, or making a reservation for a few weeks from now, you'll be out the money immediately. By using a credit card, you will have dispute rights that might not come with your debit card.

HOTELS

Use a credit card. Different hotels have differing policies, so ask about their policy regarding deposits and holds before you present your card. Some hotels will place holds to cover them in the event that you leave without settling the entire bill. The holds or deposits can be for amounts in the hundreds to make sure you don't run up a long distance bill, empty the mini bar or trash the room. Holds are almost unnoticeable if you're using credit, but can be an issue for debit cards where your checking account may only have enough to cover what you need.

GAS STATIONS / GROCERY STORES

Use a debit card. Use cash. Some gas stations offer a discount for cash, but not debit cards. If you use your debit card, pay at the pump and select the PIN number option which should debit only the amount you've actually spent. If you don't pay at the pump and don't have cash, use a credit card. But be aware that some gas stations might place a hold for more than the amount you requested in case you are one of those customers who leaves without paying.

Congratulations!

Congratulations! You have completed Your Personal Money Diary. It's quite a commitment to make, and you should be proud of yourself. You should now have an in-depth understanding of your expenses, debts and income. Now that you understand your lifestyle and the amount you need to maintain it, the next step is to make sure you're prepared for retirement and can truly enjoy your retirement years.

Whether you're planning on retiring in 10, 15, or 20 years from now or you're already retired, this information can mean the difference between living a comfortable retirement or just barely getting by. Don't let inflation, taxes, wrong investments and all the other economical factors sneak up on you and steal away your hard earned dollars.

Call one of our Personal Money Trainers today at 888-PLJ-2525 / 888-755-2525 and set up your complimentary assessment so you can get started on the right retirement path.

"Money grows on
the tree of persistence."

~Japanese Proverb